the MAGIC of MINDSET

THE
magic
of
mindset

A JOURNAL TO GET UNSTUCK

JOHANNA WRIGHT

Andrews McMeel
PUBLISHING®

THIS BOOK IS DEDICATED TO:

GABE, ADRIANA, PATTY, MATT,
FELICITY, + JENNY.
THANK YOU FOR BELIEVING in this
so I could, too.

INTRODUCTION

HELLO! WELCOME! I'm so glad YOU'RE HERE.

IF YOU'RE FEELING stuck IN ONE (OR SEVERAL) AREAS OF YOUR LIFE, YOU'RE IN THE RIGHT PLACE!

I BELIEVE OUR PURPOSE ON EARTH is TO KNOW AND SHARE OUR TRUE SELVES. I think THAT'S WHY FEELING STUCK CAN FEEL SO BAD. WE KNOW WE'RE MEANT TO GROW, BUT OLD BELIEFS AND FALSE ASSUMPTIONS ABOUT OURSELVES CAN KEEP US IN A STUCK PATTERN.

I CREATED this JOURNAL TO HELP MYSELF OUT OF A REALLY STUCK PLACE. I KEPT READING ABOUT THE CONCEPT OF MINDSET, AND IT REALLY RESONATED. I STARTED ILLUSTRATING SOME MINDSET CONCEPTS TO HELP MYSELF UNDERSTAND AND ABSORB THEM IN A CREATIVE WAY. THE PROCESS really HELPED ME SHIFT SOME THOUGHT AND FEELING HABITS THAT WERE KEEPING ME FROM MOVING FORWARD. I STILL USE THE TOOLS IN THIS JOURNAL TO CONNECT WITH MY TRUE SELF EVERY DING, DANG DAY!

WHAT THE HECK DOES

MINDSET

even mean?

THE NOUN mindset WAS FIRST USED in the '30s TO MEAN "HABITS of MIND FORMED BY PREVIOUS EXPERIENCE." PSYCHOLOGIST CAROL DWECK has spent her ENTIRE career STUDYING AND POPULARIZING THE CONCEPT of "FIXED MINDSET" AND "GROWTH MINDSET." HER RESEARCH has REVEALED WHAT you BELIEVE AFFECTS WHAT YOU ACHIEVE.

YOUR MIND habits AND PERSPECTIVES ARE PART conscious, PART UNCONSCIOUS, AND can BE learned AND UNLEARNED. THE GOAL OF this JOURNAL is TO GUIDE YOUR conscious and UNCONSCIOUS MIND THROUGH the CHANGE PROCESS, using YOUR own CREATIVITY, imagination, and UNIVERSAL GUIDANCE.

MY BRAIN REALLY RESPONDED TO THE CREATIVE PRACTICES in this JOURNAL, AND I BELIEVE YOURS WILL, TOO!

Imagine your MIND AS A WILD LANDSCAPE READY To BE EXPLORED

THINGS YOU'LL USE IN THIS JOURNAL

MAGIC WAND ↱

INNER CRYSTAL BALL ↙

FUTURE SELF

inner GUIDANCE

QUIET REFLECTION + IMAGINATION

↪ EXPLORATION

THE POWER of IMAGINATION makes US infinite.

— JOHN MUIR

GET CURIOUS. GO DEEP.
FEEL. EXPLORE.
LET GO. CREATE NEW
paths....

— YOU GOT THIS.

thanks, BIRDIE.

5

LIST the PLACES in YOUR LIFE WHERE YOU FEEL STUCK. USE
MORE SPACE IF YOU NEED.

YOU MUST DO THE THING you THINK YOU CANNOT DO.

— ELEANOR ROOSEVELT

IMAGINE LOOKING BACK A YEAR FROM NOW ON THE LIST OF PLACES YOU FEEL STUCK. YOU'VE COMPLETELY RESOLVED ONE thing ON THAT list. WHAT ARE YOU MOST PROUD OF TRANSFORMING?

write
YOUR OWN ENDING

IF this STUCK PLACE in YOUR LIFE WAS a CHAPTER in A BOOK, HOW WOULD YOU LIKE IT TO END?

observe your BEHAVIOR

TRY imagining YOU are A GIANT quietly WATCHING the BEHAVIOR OF LITTLE YOU throughout YOUR DAY.

observations

OBSERVE YOUR BEHAVIOR WHEN YOU'RE FEELING STUCK or
POWERLESS. WHAT ACTIONS DO YOU TAKE?
YOU DON'T HAVE to change anything, JUST PRACTICE NOTICING.

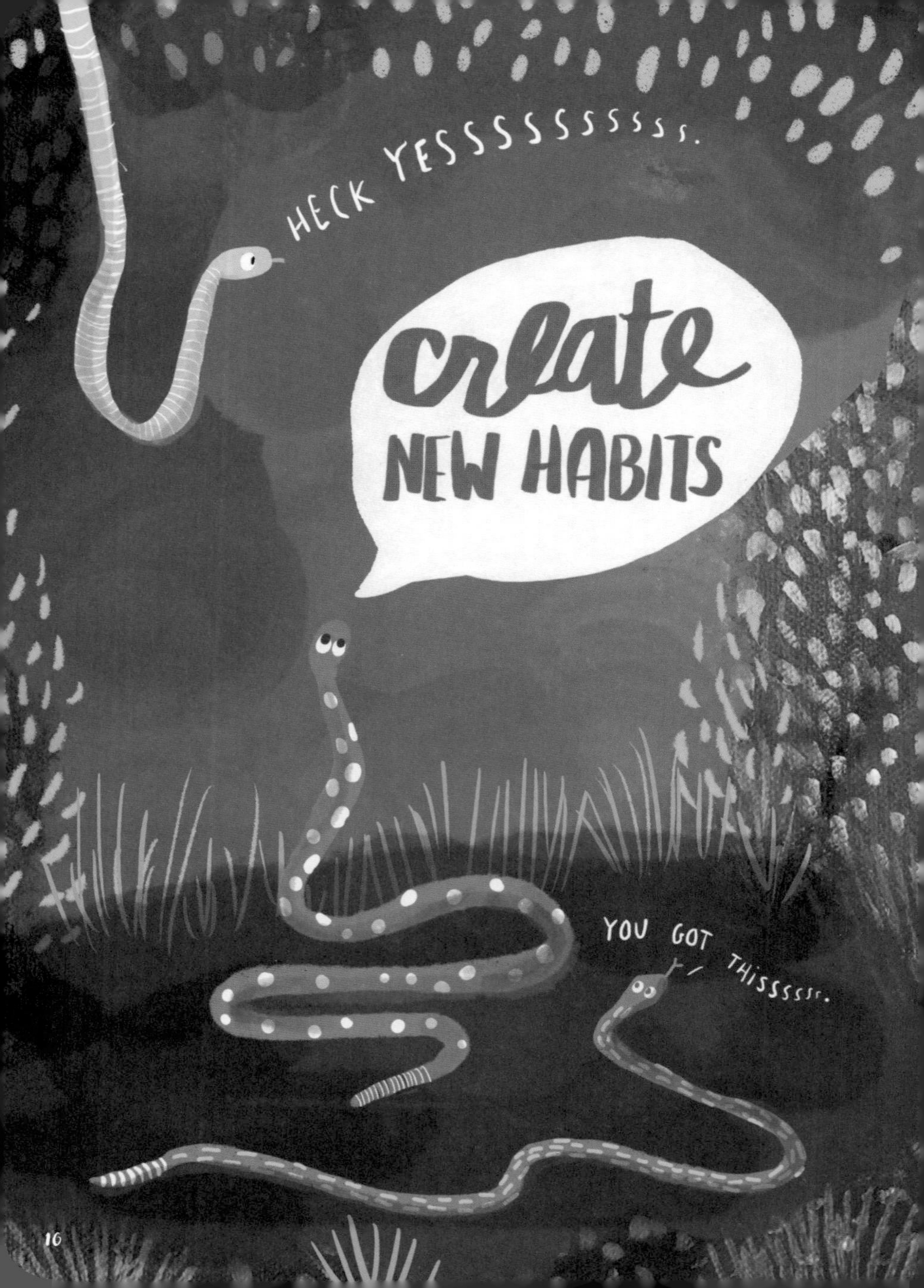
HECK YESSSSSSSSSSSS.
create
NEW HABITS
YOU GOT THISSSSSS.

CAN YOU THINK OF A BEHAVIOR THAT NO LONGER SERVES YOU BUT YOU KEEP REPEATING? DESCRIBE IT BELOW.

THE discomfort THAT comes WHEN we
stop DOING A HABITUAL behavior is
KIND of LIKE WALKING through A DARK
tunnel. IT'S OK to KEEP moving. IT's
OK TO ASK for HELP. IT'S OK TO BE
UNCOMFORTABLE. IT's OK to WATCH all of
THE creatures AND BRAMBLES you ENCOUNTER
AND to keep on walking.

WHAT OBSTACLES DO YOU ANTICIPATE WHEN YOU STOP A BEHAVIOR YOU'VE BEEN WANTING to STOP? How will you navigate these obstacles?

FUTURE YOU

IMAGINE a FUTURE YOU that is COMPLETELY FREE of THE THING that's KEEPING YOU STUCK. What is it like for you? WHERE are you? WHAT are you DOING? What does it smell like? WHAT DOES IT FEEL like?

RESISTANCE is A NORMAL PART OF THE PROCESS.

LIST all of the REASONS WHY IT FEELS impossible
TO LET GO OF YOUR OLD MINDSET AND MOVE out OF the
stuck PLACE.

DREAM, REFLECT, GROW

THINK OF A PERSON (REAL OR IMAGINED) WITH THE MINDSET YOU DESIRE. HOW DO YOU IMAGINE they SPEND THEIR DAY? WHAT DO THEY DO FOR FUN?

asking for guidance

IMAGINE YOU FEEL the LOVING PRESENCE OF SOMEONE (REAL OR IMAGINED—OR BOTH!)

TRY WRITING A QUESTION TO THIS PERSON AND THEN WRITING the ANSWER AS FAST AS YOU CAN.

FUTURE you
wants
NOW you
TO SUCCEED

YES!

REALLY?

TRY HAVING A CONVERSATION WITH YOUR FUTURE
SELF ABOUT A BEHAVIOR YOU WANT TO STOP. WHAT
ADVICE DOES YOUR FUTURE SELF HAVE FOR YOU?

you are
WHOLE

LIST THE FEELINGS, ACTIONS, AND BELIEFS YOU WOULD
LIKE TO LET GO OF.

WHAT ACTIONS COULD YOU TAKE TO GET unstuck?

WHAT MASSIVE ACTIONS COULD YOU TAKE? THINK **BIG**.

GO BIG!

CAN YOU BREAK the massive actions DOWN TO
TINIER MICROSTEPS?

SLOW
+
STEADY!

align with YOUR inner guidance

ASK YOURSELF, "IS THERE ANYTHING I NEED TO KNOW RIGHT NOW?"

WHAT ACTIONS DO YOU TAKE WHEN YOU'RE AVOIDING YOUR FEELINGS?
SHhhhhhhhh....
TOO BUSY SCROLLING...

LIST ALL OF THE ACTIONS YOU TAKE WHEN YOU'RE AVOIDING YOUR FEELINGS. (NON-ACTION CAN BE AN ACTION!)

ARE THERE ACTIONS YOU AVOID TAKING BECAUSE OF THE WAY
YOU FEEL WHEN YOU TAKE them?

LIST ALL OF the ACTIONS AND ASSOCIATED FEELINGS
YOU CAN THINK of.

create
A SAFE
HAVEN
in your
MIND.

on it!

DESCRIBE A PLACE (REAL OR IMAGINED) WHERE YOU FEEL PEACEFUL AND SAFE.

WHAT ACTIONS COULD YOU TAKE TO GENERATE
THE FEELINGS YOU WANT TO HAVE?

ANCHOR

YOURSELF WITH *your* SENSES.

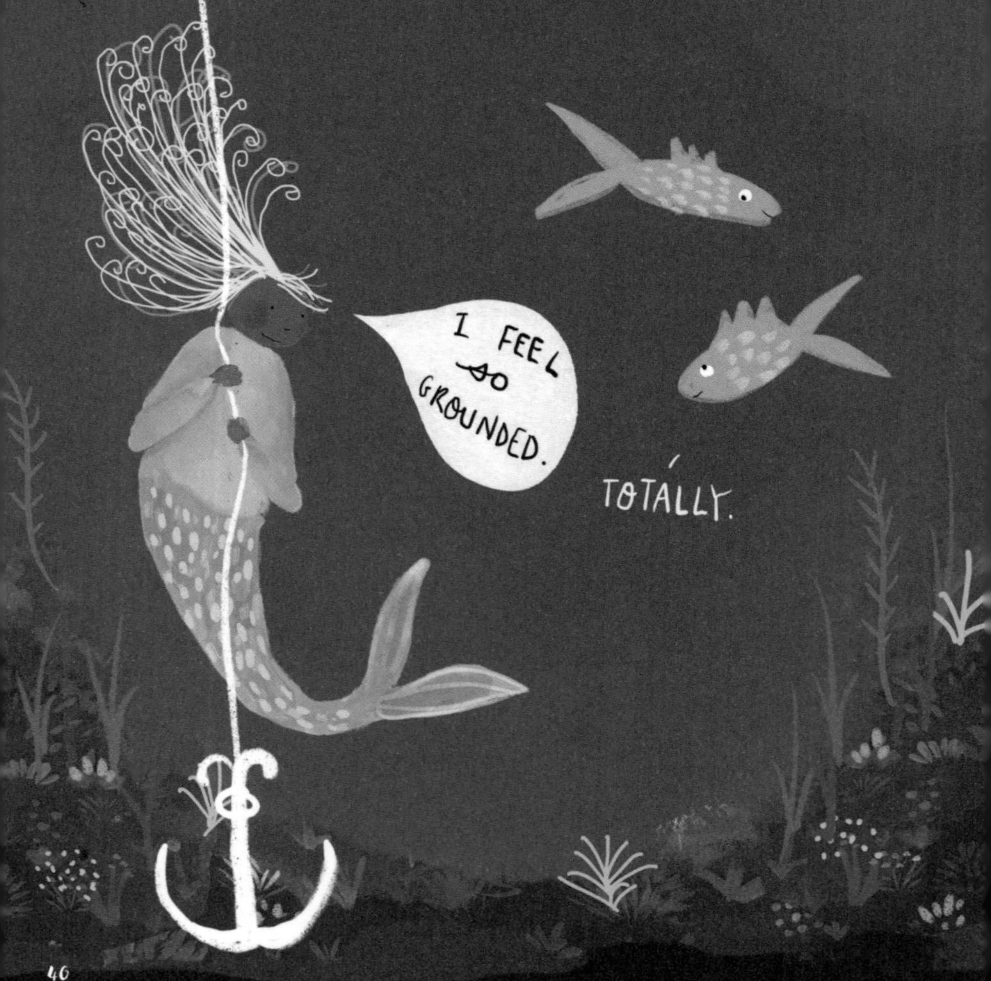

MAKE A LIST OF SENSORY EXPERIENCES THAT YOU ENJOY.
WHAT DO YOU MOST LOVE TO SEE? TASTE? TOUCH? SMELL? HEAR?

BODY
scan

CLOSE YOUR EYES. GET STILL. imagine WARM, MELTED BUTTER POURING in THROUGH THE top OF YOUR HEAD. FEEL it slowly MELT tension in YOUR WHOLE BODY.

WHERE DO YOU HOLD TENSION AND EMOTION IN YOUR BODY? WHERE IN YOUR BODY DO YOU FEEL EMOTIONS LIKE FEAR, ANGER, AND GRIEF?

FOCUS ON A PART
OF YOUR BODY THAT
HURTS OR FEELS TENSE.
ASK IT, "WHAT ARE YOU
TRYING TO TELL ME? HOW CAN
I HELP YOU?"

MAKE YOUR FEELINGS
BIGGER

TRY GROWING A FEELING YOU HAVE AS BIG AS
POSSIBLE. FOCUS ON THE FEELING IN YOUR BODY.
SEE IF YOU CAN GROW THAT FEELING TO BE
AS BIG AS THE TOWN, AS BIG AS THE
COUNTRY, AS BIG AS THE UNIVERSE.
FEEL *the* BIGNESS. ALLOW IT TO
TAKE UP LOTS OF SPACE.

you are

SO
loved

LIST ALL OF THE PLACES IN YOUR LIFE WHERE YOU
FEEL DEEPLY LOVED.

HOW CAN YOU NURTURE AND CARE FOR YOURSELF
THROUGH _this_ MINDSET TRANSFORMATION PROCESS?

FORGIVENESS

IMAGINE A SITUATION OR PERSON IN YOUR LIFE THAT YOU WOULD LIKE TO FORGIVE (EVEN IF THAT PERSON IS YOURSELF). NOW PICTURE *the most loving* BEING (REAL OR IMAGINED) STANDING BEHIND YOU. THEY'RE BEAMING *so much* LOVE TO YOU. THEY LOVE YOU SO COMPLETELY AND YOU FEEL THAT LOVE IN EVERY CELL OF YOUR BODY. THE BEAM OF THAT LOVE PASSES THROUGH YOU TO THE PERSON/SITUATION YOU WOULD LIKE TO FORGIVE. FEEL HOW SAFE AND SUPPORTED YOU ARE. FEEL THE LOVE RADIATING THROUGH YOU. WATCH IT FILL UP THE PERSON/SITUATION YOU'RE FORGIVING. YOU'RE SO SAFE. YOU'RE SO *loved.*

IS there SOMEONE IN YOUR LIFE YOU'D LIKE to FORGIVE? HOW WOULD YOUR LIFE BE DIFFERENT IF YOU DID?

call back YOUR ENERGY

THINK OF A SITUATION (PERSON, EVENT, ...) WHERE YOU'VE INVESTED A LOT OF EMOTIONAL ENERGY AND WISHED YOU HADN'T. IMAGINE YOU HAVE A GIANT *MAGNET that can* RETRIEVE *it* ALL. WATCH and FEEL YOUR BEAUTIFUL, PERSONAL POWER FLOWING BACK TO YOU *through* TIME AND SPACE.

TAKIN' CHARGE

BEING awesome

LIST PEOPLE, MEMORIES, OR SITUATIONS WHERE YOU'RE CALLING YOUR ENERGY BACK.

TAKE A WALK THROUGH YOUR EMOTIONS

IMAGINE YOU'RE A TINY EXPLORER HIKING through
YOUR BODY, SEARCHING FOR THE EMOTIONS YOU
FEEL AROUND BEING STUCK. WHAT DO YOU DISCOVER?

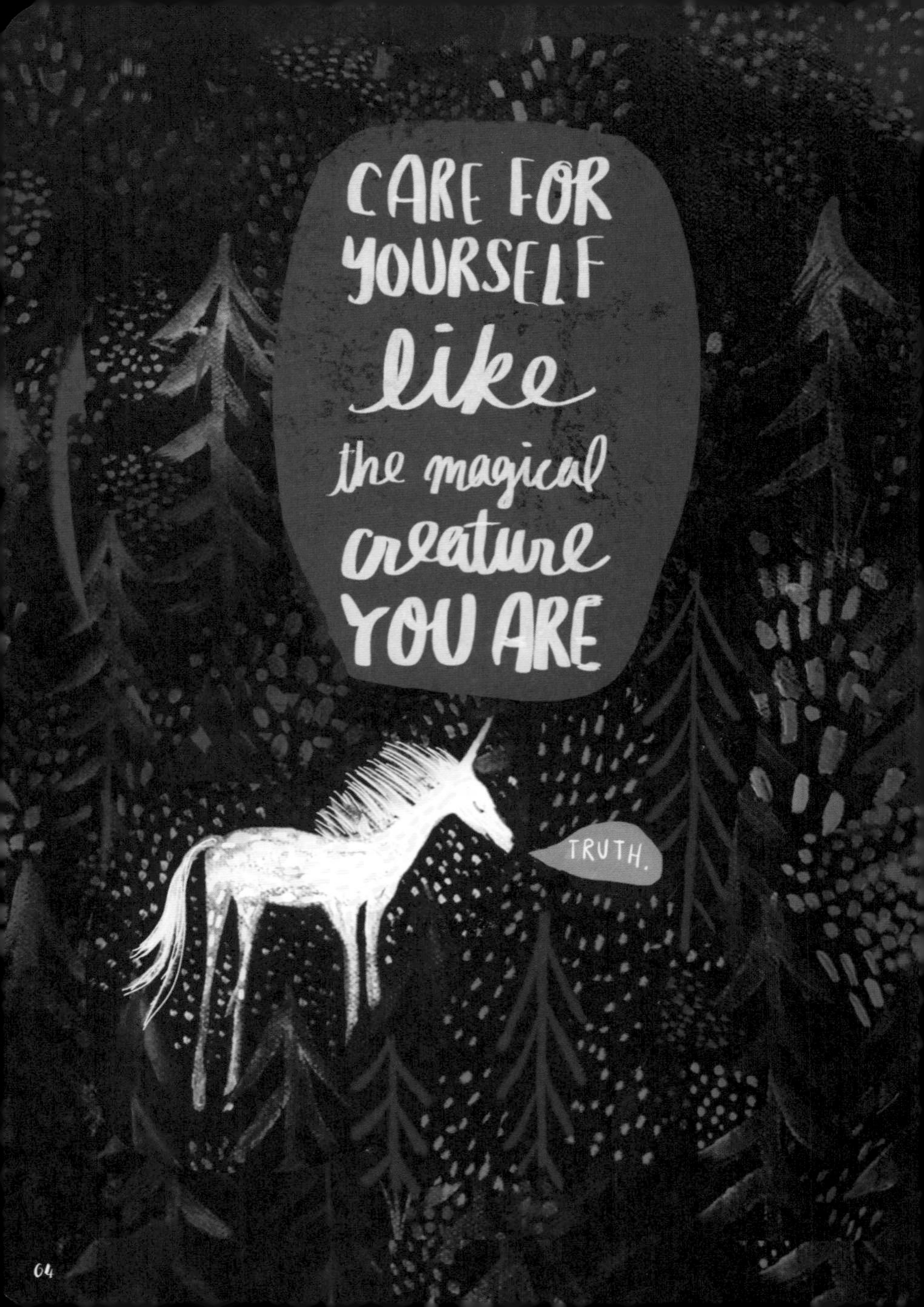
CARE FOR YOURSELF like the magical creature YOU ARE
TRUTH.

WHAT WOULD YOU DO IF YOU FOUND A SWEET
ANIMAL STUCK IN DEEP MUD? DESCRIBE HOW YOU
WOULD RESCUE IT AND CARE FOR IT. FEEL ALL
OF THE EMPATHY AND CONCERN YOU WOULD HAVE.

Can You TRANSFER Some OF THAT LOVE
AND CARE to THE STUCK part of Yourself?

CLEAR STUCK emotion

IMAGINE YOU HAVE A VACUUM cleaner
THAT CAN CLEAR stuck EMOTION.
PLACE YOUR HAND OVER THE PART
OF YOUR BODY THAT FEELS TENSE.
PICTURE your HAND as the
VACUUM, removing and CLEARING
stuck ENERGY all the WAY
DOWN TO YOUR CELLS. FOCUS DEEPLY
ON YOUR FEELINGS as they RELEASE.
OFFER the OLD EMOTION TO THE
UNIVERSE OR A LOVING PRESENCE.

DESCRIBE YOUR EXPERIENCE WITH CLEARING STUCK
emotion. WHAT HAS WORKED FOR YOU IN THE PAST?

it is by going

DOWN

into the

abyss

that we

RECOVER

the treasures

of life.

—JOSEPH CAMPBELL

IMAGINE YOUR MIND AS A ROCKY LANDSCAPE. YOU ARE
A BRAVE EXPLORER AND YOU ENTER THE SCARIEST CAVE.
YOU SHINE YOUR LIGHT INTO THE DARKEST, CREEPIEST
CORNER. WHAT DO YOU FIND?

CLOSE YOUR EYES AND IMAGINE A TREASURE CHEST
THAT CONTAINS A PROBLEM IN YOUR LIFE YOU
WOULD LIKE TO SOLVE. OPEN the CHEST AND
PULL THINGS OUT. KEEP PULLING things OUT
UNTIL YOU'VE FOUND SOMETHING that SHIFTS
YOUR PERSPECTIVE AND EMOTION. OPEN YOUR EYES
AND DESCRIBE IT BELOW.

DIG
DOWN
deep
AND
EXPLORE
your
root
thoughts

HEY...

Hi...

TRY HAVING A WRITTEN CONVERSATION WITH THE ROOT THOUGHTS THAT ARE HOLDING YOU BACK. IF YOU'RE NOT SURE WHAT THEY ARE, TRY ASKING THEM TO REVEAL THEMSELVES WHILE YOU WRITE.

snakes in
THE GRASS

OLD thought PATTERNS CAN BE hard to OBSERVE Sometimes. WE CAN STARTLE them TO THE SURFACE of OUR MINDS BY taking MASSIVE ACTION TOWARD OUR GOAL....

PICTURE YOURSELF TAKING MASSIVE ACTION TOWARD A DREAM.
IMAGINE WHAT IT WOULD FEEL LIKE IN FULL DETAIL, THEN LIST ANY
NEGATIVE THOUGHTS THAT POP UP IN RESPONSE.

time TRAVEL

THINK BACK to A PLACE in YOUR life WHEN YOU NEEDED MORE SUPPORT.

IT COULD BE FROM YOUR CHILDHOOD or YESTERDAY. CLOSE your eyes + travel BACK to this time. OBSERVE the younger You. Embrace the younger You + tell them everything You NEEDED to hear BACK THEN.

DESCRIBE YOUR TIME TRAVEL EXPERIENCE. WHAT DID YOU TELL YOUR YOUNGER SELF?

LIST ALL OF THE KIND THINGS YOU NEED TO HEAR THE MOST.

YOU
have all
the answers

YOU REALLY DO HAVE ALL OF THE ANSWERS. WHAT IS SOMETHING YOU KNOW DEEP DOWN IS TRUE BUT YOU HAVEN'T FELT READY TO FACE?

new BELIEF seeds

YOU HAVE A JAR OF NEW BELIEF SEEDS READY TO BE PLANTED. LIST THE NEW BELIEFS YOU WOULD MOST LIKE TO PLANT.

planting
NEW BELIEFS

PICK THE BELIEF THAT YOU WOULD MOST LIKE TO SEE
TAKE ROOT. HOW CAN YOU TEND TO IT? HOW CAN YOU
PRACTICE THIS NEW THOUGHT?

IT'S NORMAL FOR OUR MINDS TO OFFER LOTS OF RESISTANCE AND SELF-DOUBT WHEN WE PLANT NEW THOUGHTS. SPILL ALL OF YOUR RESISTANT *thoughts* HERE.

WHAT IF?
WHAT IF?
WHAT IF?
WHAT IF?
WHAT IF?
WHAT if?
WHAT IF?
WHAT IF?
WHAT IF?
WHAT IF?
WHAT IF?
WHAT IF?
BLOOP

ASKING OURSELVES WHAT-IF QUESTIONS IS A POWERFUL TOOL FOR CHANGE. IT OPENS US TO POSSIBILITY. ASK YOURSELF WHAT-IF QUESTIONS BELOW. "WHAT IF I BELIEVED IN MYSELF?"... "WHAT IF I LET GO?"...

how did I do that?

THINK OF SOMETHING YOU'D LIKE TO DO (BUT HAVEN'T), AND ASK YOURSELF, "HOW DID I DO THAT?" LET THE ANSWER FLOW BELOW.

CREATING NEW BELIEFS
CAN BE HARD FOR OUR
MINDS TO ACCEPT.
ACCLIMATING TO THE
NEW BELIEF IS A PROCESS.
TRY WRITING YOUR OLD
BELIEF AT THE BOTTOM
OF THE MOUNTAIN AND
YOUR NEW BELIEF AT THE
TOP. IF YOU FEEL RESISTANCE
TO YOUR NEW BELIEF, TRY
PRACTICING MORE NEUTRAL
STATEMENTS ALONG THE WAY.

PRETEND the NEXT THING YOU DRINK IS ACTUALLY A MAGIC POTION THAT ROCKETS YOU OUT OF STUCKNESS. HOW WILL YOU SPEND YOUR DAY?

LIST EVERYTHING THAT'S WILDLY INTERESTING TO YOU RIGHT NOW, EVEN IF IT'S WEIRD OR EMBARRASSING.

DESCRIBE A PERSON (REAL OR IMAGINED) WHO EMBODIES THE MINDSET YOU WANT TO CREATE. HOW DO they BEHAVE? What are they like?

WHAT QUESTIONS DO YOU HAVE FOR YOUR FUTURE SELF?
FOR THE UNIVERSE? TRY GETTING STILL, CONNECTING WITH
YOUR QUESTIONS, AND ALLOWING the ANSWERS TO FLOW.

THE UNIVERSE DOESN'T ALLOW PERFECTION.

— STEPHEN HAWKING

WHEW....

LIST THE PLACES in YOUR LIFE WHERE IT FEELS
like PERFECTIONISM is SLOWING YOU DOWN.

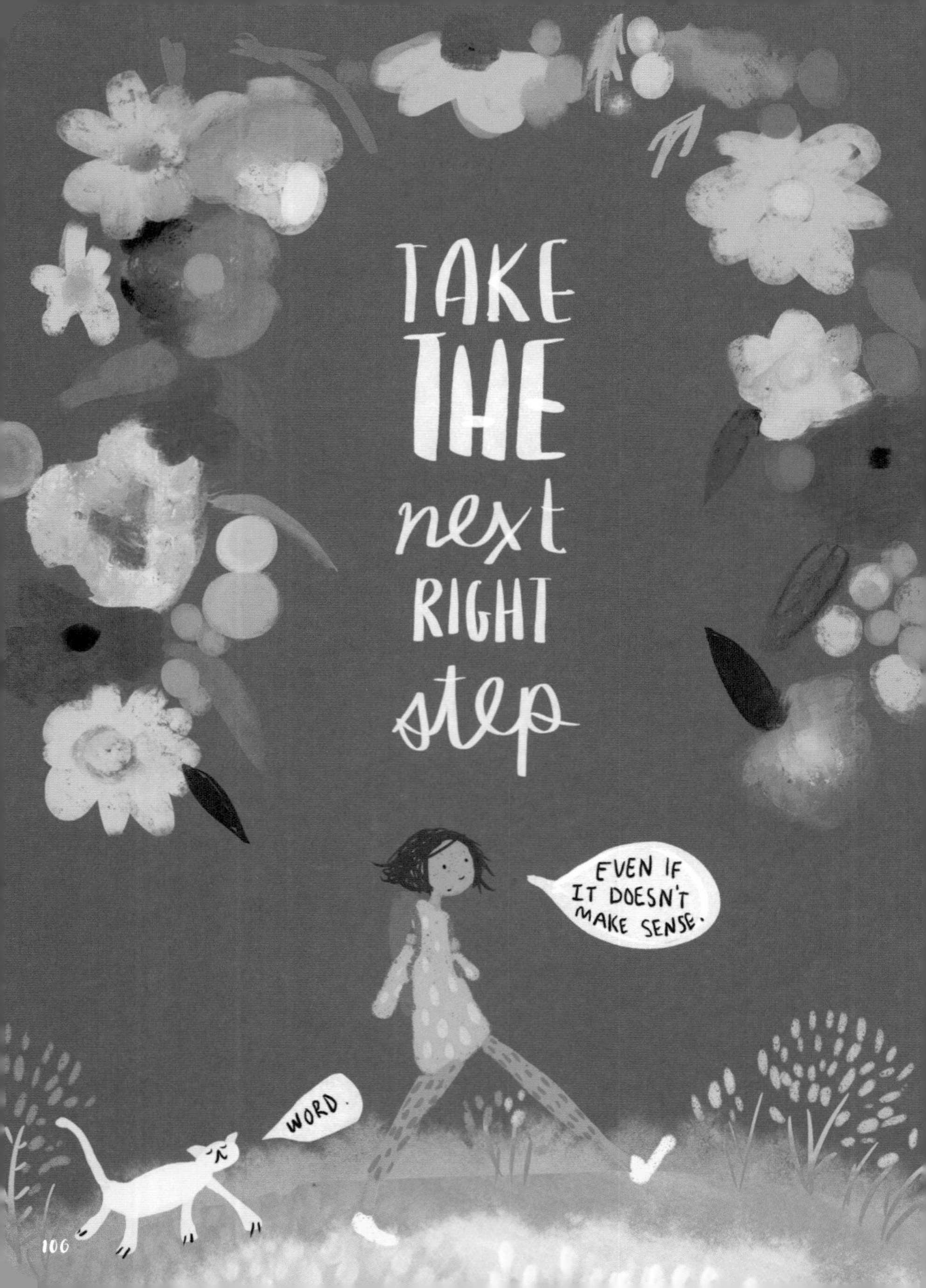
TAKE THE next RIGHT step
EVEN IF IT DOESN'T MAKE SENSE.
WORD.

WHAT ARE THE NEXT RIGHT ACTION STEPS FOR YOU?

CAN YOU BREAK THAT NEXT RIGHT STEP INTO MICROSTEPS?

Oh YEAH.

walking through INDECISION

IF YOU'RE STRUGGLING WITH INDECISION, TRY GIVING YOURSELF
A TIME LIMIT. TELL YOURSELF, "I WILL MAKE A FINAL
CHOICE IN _____ AMOUNT OF TIME."

PICK ONE THING YOU'RE FEELING INDECISIVE ABOUT. WRITE
AS FAST AS YOU CAN ALL OF YOUR THOUGHTS AND
FEELINGS ABOUT IT.

MAGIC
is
flowing
THROUGH
YOU

IMAGINE YOU'RE BEING INTERVIEWED BY YOUR FAVORITE MAGAZINE. DESCRIBE THAT INTERVIEW BELOW.

IF YOUR SHIP DOESN'T COME IN — swim out TO IT!

—JONATHAN WINTERS

LIST the BIGGEST, MOST DRAMATIC STEPS YOU
COULD TAKE TO REACH YOUR GOAL.

cultivate

LASER

focus

KAZAM!

YOU CAN CULTIVATE THE PRACTICE OF LASER FOCUS BY TAKING ACTION FOR SMALL AMOUNTS OF TIME. MAKE A LIST OF FIVE-MINUTE ACTION STEPS. USE A TIMER TO HELP YOU FOCUS ON COMPLETING YOUR TINY TASKS.

THE MAGIC YOU'VE UNCOVERED in this JOURNAL is ALWAYS WITH YOU. YOU CAN REPEAT YOUR FAVORITE EXERCISES ANYTIME YOU WANT.

TRY WRITING A THANK-YOU NOTE TO YOURSELF BELOW, FOR YOUR WILLINGNESS TO OBSERVE, ACCEPT, LET GO, AND TRANSFORM OLD PATTERNS.

Andrews McMeel Publishing
a division of Andrews McMeel Universal
1130 Walnut Street, Kansas City, Missouri 64106

www.andrewsmcmeel.com

19 20 21 22 23 SDB 10 9 8 7 6 5 4 3 2 1

ISBN: 978-1-5248-5063-0

Library of Congress Control Number: 2019946590

Editor: Patty Rice
Art Director/Designer: Julie Barnes
Production Editor: Margaret Daniels
Production Manager: Tamara Haus

ATTENTION: SCHOOLS AND BUSINESSES
Andrews McMeel books are available at quantity discounts with
bulk purchase for educational, business, or sales promotional use.
For information, please e-mail the Andrews McMeel Publishing
Special Sales Department: specialsales@amuniversal.com.